The Morning Routine Blueprint

How to Wake Up Early, Energized and Motivated Everyday

By Mike Fishbein
www.mfishbein.com

Table of Contents

Introduction:Why A Morning Routine Will Change Your Life

I rolled out of bed and looked over at my phone. *Damn.* It was 7:36. I had hit the snooze button twice already and I was bound to be late for work *again.*

I sauntered into the shower, hoping to rinse off my hangover from the night before. It was not a success.

I got dressed, grabbed my briefcase, and headed out the door. I was already late, but I couldn't be a functioning human being until I got my coffee. While I waited in line, I couldn't help but notice the bubbly barista, smiling at everyone as she took their orders.

"I wish I could be that energetic in the morning." I thought to myself.

I got my large coffee and a muffin and was on my way.

"Have a great Saturday!", she sang in my direction.

I had completely forgotten it was the weekend. The days were blending together. I bit into my muffin. I could feel my stomach getting fatter with each bite. It was then when I knew I needed a change.

This was 2010, a time when most of my mornings were filled with caffeine and misery. By 9 or 10AM, I was a functioning human being again, but until then, I was a zombie. I'd wake up everyday "hoping" that it would be a happy and productive day.

By evening, I would realize that today just wasn't the day and I'd head out for some drinks with my friends. Alcohol would give me the energy I craved, leading me to stay out even later and eventually causing a never ending cycle of sleep deprivation.

Now that I look back, I realize I was spoiling the most productive and energetic time of the day, **the morning**.

Instead of using it to my advantage, I was spending it in a state of trance. Now, the morning is when I get the bulk of my productive work done. I now have a morning routine that turns everyday into a productive and exciting one. And I want to show you how to do the same.

Become More Productive With This Morning Ritual

Do you struggle to get out of bed and get going? Do you wish you were excited to get out of bed in the mornings? What if you could miraculously wake up tomorrow and any—or every, area of your life was transformed?

How would life be different? Would you be happier? Healthier? More successful? Which of your problems would be solved?

What if I told you that there is a "not-so-obvious" secret that is guaranteed to transform any—or literally every, area of your life, faster than you ever thought possible? What if I told you it would only take 6 minutes a day?

Enter *The Morning Routine Blueprint.* What's now being practiced by thousands of people around the world could perhaps be the simplest approach to creating the life you've always wanted.

A big reason most people aren't successful is they fail to follow a daily routine. Instead, they start each day, "hoping" they will have enough time to make progress on their goals.

If you closely examined the world's most successful people, you'd see that they start each day in an energized state, ready to accomplish any goal. What's their secret?

Like brushing your teeth, once you get in the habit of doing something, it no longer becomes a task, it's just something you do. Successful people are able to focus on their tasks because they have already built habits into their morning.

Are you tired of living a reactive kind of life rather than a proactive one? Do you want to determine how productive your day is? Do you want to find energy and happiness in your day-to-day activities?

If you do, then this is the perfect book to read.

How you start your day determines how your day will be, as well as how your day will end. Most people may not put so much thought into it, however, if you want to live a productive, happy and healthy life, you need to have a suitable morning ritual. Your morning ritual will put you in the right state mentally, physically and emotionally so that you can have the successful day you want. I know, it sounds daunting, but bare with me.

Remember the first time you went to middle school and had to wake up slightly earlier? It sucked for a month, didn't it? But, then what happened? *You adjusted.* Next thing you know, waking up an hour or two earlier wasn't so bad. It didn't become fun or easy, but it *was something you got used to.* Morning routines work the same way.

There are SO many different types of morning rituals. While everyone may have a different morning ritual, some will prove to be quite helpful while others may be detrimental. The key is to find what works best for you. That's why I wrote this book and that's why you're reading it!

Take it from me, someone who has been there without a plan and tried nearly everything.The secrets contained in this book were not pulled out of thin air. They took a lot of time and trial and error to develop. It resulted in many fatigued days, many hours wasted, and many mental struggles. Now, you are lucky enough to have them all at your disposal!

Finding the Perfect Morning Routine For You

Since 2010, through trial and error, I've found my perfect morning routine. Three times actually.

I've tried so many different strategies and rituals. Like everything in life, morning routines change along with our preferences and priorities. Along the way, I tried a lot of things. Some were awesome. Others were really weird.

Everything I've written about I know from personal experience. On top of that, I also mention some of the practices I've tried that haven't worked. Some of what I tried had a negative effect on my overall health and/or well-being. I've also included several ideas that I hope to try at some point in the future. All that being said, it's up to you to decide which methods best fit your life and preferences.

I've condensed years of experimentation into this book. You don't have to fail the way I've failed! You don't have to figure out what works and what doesn't.

Everyone is different, so you may need to see what exactly works best for you -- but what's included in this book has been tremendously beneficial to me. I know it will be for you, too.

I've also included some bonus chapters on additional productivity life hacks that will help you live a better and healthier life as a whole.

There are so many great habits and mindsets you can maintain to increase your energy and boost your productivity. Having a strong morning routine is just one of them. Read through to the end of this book where you'll discover some tips and resources and you'll know exactly what I mean.

I describe three different morning routines in the first three chapters. First, I'll give you a brief overview of each morning routine so you can visualize it as a whole. Then, I'll go back and break it down for you, allowing you to understand every aspect of it. I will explain every precise detail and include everything you'll need to know about it, why it helps, and how to do it effectively.

In this book, I also lay out the importance of a night routine. I talk about my weekend routine, and how to have a fun and productive weekend without making the Monday morning transition difficult.

I cover all of this plus a lot more. So, without further ado, let's get started!

About the Author

Hi there. I am a self-published author and a content marketing expert. I've written multiple books on entrepreneurship and marketing. I've worked with startups and fortune 500 companies on content marketing and product management. I've had my writing featured on sites such as *Entrepreneur*, *Huffington Post* and *The Next Web*. Previously, I worked at a tech startup in New York doing marketing and product management.

The following book contains the strategies and tactics I've used to find the perfect morning routine, and I want to help others do the same.

Feel free to check out my personal development newsletter at mfishbein.com and my books at mfishbein.com/amazon.

Additional Resources: It Doesn't Stop With A Morning Routine

Having a morning routine is amazing, but it can also serve as the perfect stepping stone to improve other aspects of your life.

For example, have you always hated the term "networking" even though you knew it was something you needed to do? Or, maybe you're trying not to let email and social media control you but you don't know what apps to use?

As much as this book includes dozens of other hacks worth trying, it doesn't have everything. If you're interested in personal development and improving in other areas of your life, I've written two other books that I think you'd love.

I also have a lifehacks newsletter that I send out a few times a month. It's packed with value, and I think you'll benefit from it.

Lifehacks Newsletter

Join my community as I share my best secrets, practices, and lessons learned in order to live a better and more efficient life.

Learn about lifehacks such as:

- *How to optimize your your productivity-*
- *How to maximize creativity*
- *How to overcome procrastination as I share my best ideas*
- *How to deal with nonconformity*
- *And more!*

No B.S., just actional advice from real life experiences.

Sign up for free at mfishbein.com/life-hacks-newsletter

67 Business Productivity Apps to Make Life Easier, Maximize Your Time and Get Stuff Done

Do you feel like you're wasting time because you don't know exactly which apps to use?

The technology we have available at our fingertips for little or no cost is truly amazing. It's never been easier to increase productivity, make life easier, manage time, and automate your business marketing!

The 67 business productivity apps in this book can help you maximize and optimize your marketing, blogging, writing, entrepreneurship, and daily life outside of business. Buy the book at mfishbein.com/productivityapps

77 Lifehacks: How to Get More Energy, Increase Productivity & Be Happy

Do you feel like you should be doing more but **you don't have the energy?** Are you looking to **improve your mood and productivity?**

Do you want to live a better life and do more exciting things?

If so, then this book is for people like you. People who want to boost their mental energy. People who want **more excitement and positivity in their life**, but aren't sure how to do so. Check out the book at mfishbein.com/77lifehacks and add more excitement and positivity to your life.

Chapter 1
My Morning Routine #1: Fitness and Energy

Fall 2014.

I was so tired I could barely walk. I left the office around 10PM on Friday after a 14 hour day and a 70 hour week. I didn't even think about hanging out with my friends or doing anything fun. I hadn't taken a day off in a couple weeks. Working right through the weekends. After a long week of hard work, the only thing that sounded appealing was my bed.

I gripped my right thigh tightly with both hands. I lifted my leg with my arms and tossed it a few inches in front of where I had picked it up. Then I switched to the other leg. It took every ounce of my physical and mental energy to even take a step. I never thought something so simple could be so hard.

To maximize my time and energy for working I cut down on cooking healthy food and stopped going to the gym. I was going to Popeye's fried chicken a couple times per week because it was fast, cheap, and close to my office.

My formerly toned body turned to mush. My mood and energy levels began to drop. I didn't have the energy to work out.

So I didn't.

At the time, I thought I was "saving my energy". But spending time working out and eating healthy would have given me more energy to work. It was a downward spiral that I needed to cut off.

Working out and eating healthy creates and boosts your energy. It is more than worthy of the investment...

Knowing I needed to get myself back on the wagon, I instituted a new morning routine...

Morning Routine #1 Benefits: Fitness and Energy

This was a routine that would put conditions in my life that would make it more likely for me to actually get to the gym. A routine that would give me lasting energy and a better mood for the rest of my busy work day.

By going to the gym first thing in the morning, my day started off with an accomplishment. I got out of bed and went straight to the gym. I got a strange sense of pride knowing that my roommates, and probably most other people in the world, were not able to do it.

I knew if I put the gym later in the day, I would find a reason not to go. At 7AM, no one is calling me. Nothing needs to be turned in. No excuses.

This routine helped me massively increase my productivity, boost my energy levels, improve my mood, and strengthen myself physically. This morning routine is great if you want to have more energy and get in better physical shape.

If you're hoping to improve your physique while still being productive at work, then I recommend considering the actions of this routine.

Let's take a look.

Morning routine #1:

6:00AM: Wake up to Music
6:10AM: Drink Water
6:30AM: Walk to the Gym
7:00AM: Exercise
8:00AM: Shower
8:15AM: Breakfast + Vitamin Stack
8:45AM: Arrive at the Office, Coffee/Tea
8:55AM: Write Down 10 ideas
9:10AM: Work on Most Important Task
10:00AM: Check Email+ News
10:45AM: Check Other Tasks, Write Down to-do List and Ideas
11:00AM: Work

As you can see, this routine was pretty long. While on paper it seems ridiculous to follow the same five hour routine every morning, but I assure you that it's worth it.

With this routine, I was able to reach my physical goals while also improving my productivity at work. And, though it may seem mundane and repetitive to do this everyday, I guarantee you that everyday was not the same. Some days I may have showered for an extra two minutes, other days I spent more time writing out my ideas. It doesn't have to be 100% spot on every day. I'm not perfect. No one is.

Below, I describe each component in more detail, including how to practice each ritual and how it can benefit you. For simplicity purposes, I've written it in present tense.

1. Wake up to Music

6:00AM

The music is clutch here. The typical alarm clock sound is miserable. When I hear it in a movie or on TV, it makes me cringe. If you use your phone as an alarm clock and someone uses that tone as their ringtone, it makes you cringe. Why? Because you associate with the feelings that come with waking up. Waking up to the standard alarm clock sounds is a terrible way to start the day. It makes the first thought that pops into your head every morning a negative one.

Instead, I set my alarm clock to play the music of my choice. I use a speaker dock that connects to my Apple products. I connect it to my old school ipod so that I don't have to keep my phone in my room.

I usually set my alarm clock to play funk music. That way, the first thought that pops into my head every morning is a pleasant one. The sweet sounds of nasty funk brings me joy and makes me want to dance. You can't sleep when you're dancing. You can barely refrain from smiling either. And, I have less desire to turn off my alarm clock because the sounds are so pleasant. The result is that I'm out of bed faster and in a better mood. One of my favorites that never gets old is "Your Love Keeps Liftin Me Higher" by Jackie Wilson.

I've also tried putting my alarm clock away from my bed so I have to get up and walk over to turn it off. This has worked fairly well for me. Though I typically don't have a problem getting up after my alarm clock goes off when it is next to me. Once my alarm is off, I don't have a problem getting out of bed, so getting up and walking to turn it off didn't make much of a difference. So I don't use this strategy, but it might be useful for you if you're the type who likes to hit 'snooze' multiple times.

I also want to add that it's important to plan something fun in the mornings. When your morning is filled with boring and mundane tasks, you have no incentive to wake up. For me, going to the gym is a pleasurable activity. I enjoy it and I know it's good for me. So, it made it easier to wake up knowing I was going to listen to great music and work out.

Some other ideas for fun things in the morning are going on a walk outside, reading, meeting someone for breakfast, or a Skype call catching up with a friend on the other side of the world. You'd be surprised at how much easier it is to get out of bed when you have something to look forward to. It's also a great way to start your day, doing something fun and exciting.

2. Drink Water (eat breakfast later)

6:10AM

Almost immediately after waking up, I drink a cup of water. I typically don't drink much water at night, but after sleeping for eight hours, my body is long overdue for some hydration. The cup of water can also suppress your appetite a bit.

Sometimes I include a scoop of BCAAs (Branch Chain Amino Acids) in the water. BCAAs have been shown to help with muscle recovery. They also give me a bit of strength and fuel for my morning workout. We'll get to my morning workout soon, don't worry. If you are not doing an extensive amount of exercising you probably do not need the BCAAs.

I typically sleep for about seven or eight hours per night and I don't eat before bed. In fact, I usually don't eat anything within a few hours of going to bed. I used to eat a small meal before bed, but I've started to make my last meal around 8pm at the absolute latest. Not eating late at night has been helping me sleep deeper and wake up more energized. I have an entire chapter dedicated to having a night routine, so we'll leave it at that for now!

I don't eat breakfast first thing in the morning because I've found it hard to consume and digest and I'm usually not that hungry. It also takes time to digest breakfast which I don't have, since I workout early in the morning. If you wake up hungry, that's fine. A light snack is more than okay. I just suggest to keep it healthy and not too heavy. Especially if you are going to exercise.

Given my slightly over-ambitious workout regimen, it can be easy for muscles to get overworked and take too long to recover. BCAAs help prevent that. If I am feeling hungry, tired, or if my muscles are sore, I add BCAAs to my water. If you are interested in BCAAs, I would recommend reading more about them on your own on a vitamin/nutrition/bodybuilding supplement site such as GNC.

I used to drink coffee first thing in the morning. I would be a zombie until I drank my first cup. My rationale for drinking caffeine first thing in the morning was that I usually feel a little groggy and slow early in the morning and I wanted to get more morning started faster. I wanted to put my day into turbo mode right from the start.

Walk to the Gym

6:30AM

After brushing my teeth and getting dressed for the day, I walk to the gym. I don't shower before I leave my apartment because I shower at the gym.

Walking to the gym is refreshing. It wakes me up and gives me more time to relax and think. In New York it's often so quiet at this time, and sometimes it's still dark out. It's a really pleasant time of the day.

I drink my coffee on the way to the gym. The caffeine gives me energy for my workout.

3. Workout at the Gym

7:00AM

By 7:00, I'm at the gym and ready to exercise.

Note: I don't have maximum energy at this time. I have the best workouts when I exercise midday. But my goal is not to get huge. I'm not a bodybuilder. My goal is to increase my energy, creative thinking, productivity, and mood. I don't plan on being a bodybuilder. I don't even need a six pack. I just want to get my blood flowing, increase my metabolism, and zone out for a bit.

Going to the gym everyday is a lot, but it keeps me in the habit. At the time, I was completely out of shape, so I had to go everyday since I had fallen off.

My workout is short. I do the same regiment five days of the week, leaving the weekends to relax or take a long walk.

While I work out, I listen to a lot of Rage Against the Machine, Smashing Pumpkins, Lightning Bolt, and other bands in that genre. This type of music helps me get energized and puts me in a good mood, which helps me be productive throughout the day.

My workout isn't anything too intense. Here's the rough outline:

junbui

10-20 mins: I stretch out my main muscles for the first five minutes. I do a few yoga poses and hold them for as long as I feel like it. Yoga is hard, but it feels great. These are the poses I do:

Child's pose
Cat/cow
Downward facing dog
Upward facing dog

I also spend about five minutes stretching out my neck because I sometimes get neck pain.

30-40 mins: I work on 2-3 muscles for the next thirty minutes. I try to hit all the main muscle groups, alternating days, so 2-3 per workout. One day I'll do biceps, back and legs. The next day, I'll do shoulders, triceps, and chest. I do 10 reps at each machine. Sometimes I do less. Some days I'll hop on the elliptical for ten minutes for some cardiovascular exercise. Again, I'm not a personal trainer, so please don't copy my workout regimen.

I know my workout routine can be better, but for what I want, it's great.

Since this routine can be a bit too much to do everyday, I take at least one day off during the weekend.

3. Shower With Music

8:00AM

I usually listen to music in the shower. Well, the music's not physically in the shower, but I can hear it while I'm showering. This is great because it boosts my mood and increases my energy levels even more. I bring my speaker dock to the shower with me - the one I use as my alarm clock. Sometimes I don't listen to music if I just want to think and relax, but most days I do.

Depending on your living situation, it may make sense to go back to your house/apartment for breakfast after the gym and shower at home. Showering at the gym saves time. It took me a while to get used to showering in a foreign bathroom, but once I got over it, it was fine. It's also a great feeling to leave the gym refreshed and ready to make the best of the rest of your day.

For convenience sake, I highly recommend choosing a gym that's located near your gym or work place. When it's far away, it's just another excuse for you to make not to go.

4. Breakfast + Vitamin Stack

8:15AM

Eating a large healthy meal is extremely important after your workout.

I eat an apple after the gym. This is pretty much the only time I have sugar. I'll also take three vitamins: Fish oil (liquid), vitamin B complex, and vitamin D.

I cook a few days worth of food at a time. Cooking is both healthier and cheaper. It's hard to find healthy food when you eat out. When you order you give yourself the opportunity to cheat. When you make a bunch of food and bring it with you, you commit to eating healthy.

I cook well rounded meals. A common batch of food for me is about a pound and a half of chicken, a can of black beans, an avocado, and some peanuts. I don't eat it all at once. I eat one meal sized portion four times throughout the day.

Notice that the meal is well rounded with protein, fat, and healthy carbohydrates. Black beans are my primary source of carbohydrates and fiber. I eat an apple that my gym provides after I workout. Other than that I just eat a lot of meat and fat. It's my own variation of the paleo or "slow carb" diet.

I was first hesitant about cutting carbohydrates out of my life completely. But once I did it, I couldn't argue with the results. I need less sleep, I feel better, and my overall energy levels are higher. I can't argue with that.

After breakfast, it's time to walk to work.

5. Arrive and Come Up with 10 Ideas

8:55AM

I want to be more creative and strategic about how I live my life. So every morning, I write down 10 ideas. They can be about anything. I write these by hand on paper.

At first, it sounded a little hokey to me. But the benefits have been profound.

It was something James Altucher had recommended doing as part of his daily practice. I've benefited from reading about his other experiences so I decided to give it a try.

I write down 10 ideas everyday as part of my morning routine. Right when I got to the office. Before I opened my computer.

The ideas are about any one topic…usually marketing ideas for my business, new business ideas, ways to improve my life or business, connections I can make between people in my network, blog post ideas, lists to include within blog posts, ways I could help people, etc.. I write using pen and paper.

Later in this book you will find a chapter on the surprising benefits I've experienced as a result of writing down 10 ideas. I'll lay out everything later on, from how to come up with the ideas, what kinds of ideas to come up with, and more.

6. Important task

9:10AM

Once I've gotten my ideas down on paper, it's time to get to work. I get started by working on one major task. If I don't have a major task for the day, then I'll complete one of a few smaller ones.

I do my best work early in the morning. At this point in time, I've cleared my thoughts, so I find it extremely easy to focus.

By then I already know what the task is and don't need to spend any extra time and energy thinking about my tasks for the day (more on that in chapter 3). I try to keep stuff outside of my head and written down somewhere.

It's always so tempting to check email. Most days I don't, but some days I do. This is one area I could definitely improve. Some days I definitely need be on top of my email, so it is more responsible I check my email, but most days I don't need to check before 10AM.

7. Email + News

10:00AM

The News

I try not to watch a lot of news. This is definitely one that you might not agree with me on. Most people believe we all have some kind of obligation to stay "informed." I do stay informed on important topics but I don't watch the news every day.

There are a couple news sources that I trust, so I watch those. In total, I probably spend about three hours per week on news. No more. The news is filled with information that won't be relevant next week.

Instead, I prefer to read educational blog posts. In my opinion there are many other things that someone could be doing instead of watching the news. I think a lot of people are addicted to the news. I experience almost no benefit, and neither does anyone else, as a result of my knowing about the latest murder or celebrity gossip.

I do follow macroeconomics and important societal issues. But I don't need to know about every detail of every politician's life or all the horrible things going on in the world that I can't do anything about.

Many of these issues are actually pretty insignificant. As horrible as it sounds, sports and political scandals are pretty insignificant. Yes, it's not good that our nation's' leaders are terrible at their jobs, but if I followed every political news story and sporting event I would have no time to live my life, be productive, or have fun. There are better things I could be doing for society and for myself.

Email

I tried doing a batched Inbox so that I don't get email outside of the times I prefer. Batched Inbox is a tool that allows you to get emails sent to you only at the specific times you choose. I chose to get email three times per day at 10am, 2pm, and 6pm.

I loved this because I've found email to be one of my biggest time sucks. I read my email, and then I respond to those emails or take action on whatever is needed, and then I get more emails, and the cycle continues.

Unfortunately, I was not able to maintain this habit. I got too nervous about people needing to reach me. It wasn't practical, since there are situations where I have an urgent client assignment or an impromptu meeting.

If if didn't need a reply right away, I would simply bookmark the email and get back to it another time.

8. Wunderlist + Set goals + Work for the rest of the day

10:45AM

After checking email and consuming the top stories, it's time to check wunderlist and see what my other tasks are for the day. I then set some goals based on my to-do list. Having a to-do list is crucial. I talk more about that in routine #3.

11:00AM

Once I've got my goals, I set deadlines for myself.

A task takes as long as it's allowed. On the days when I set deadlines, I get more done than when I have all day and all night to work.

I take a look at my weekly goals and I give myself arbitrary deadlines. For my daily goals, I set a time that I need them done by. For my weekly goals, I set a day.

How do I decide my deadlines? I make it up. If I'm late, I'm late. But, simply having a deadline gives me extra motivation and helps me get the tasks done sooner.

Key Takeaways

After falling into an unhealthy lifestyle, I couldn't take it anymore. I felt like crap everyday, and I was getting worse everyday. I implemented this morning routine to get myself back on track, and it worked like a charm! This routine was optimized for fitness and energy and I'm so happy that it worked wonderfully.

Waking up to an annoying alarm clock sound is a terrible way to start the day, so instead I woke up to some sweet funk music. This meant my day started with dancing rather than groaning. This gave me some positive momentum early on in the day.

I went to the gym everyday first thing in the morning. I knew if I didn't go soon after I woke up then I would make up excuses not to go. My goal wasn't to get extremely buff, rather to get back into shape and feel better. My plan worked, and my energy levels increased significantly after going to the gym.

After getting in the habit of coming up with 10 ideas everyday, my creativity had also improved. I felt like a completely new person. But, I wasn't done experimenting...

Chapter 2
My Morning Routine #2: Self Knowledge and Creativity

July 2014.

After forming an exercise habit, my body and mind felt better than ever. However, I knew there were some improvements I needed to make to my physical health and creativity.

I was back in shape, but I felt like my workouts weren't efficient since I didn't have high energy levels early in the morning. During my mornings, I felt as if I was just going through the motions. I wanted to spend my mornings being focused and productive and then spend the afternoon at the gym since I had more energy at that time.

But overall, I felt fine. Great, actually.

A friend of mine found out that he had the testosterone levels of an 80 year old. This scared him.

And it scared me a bit, too. He was the same age as me and we lived similar lifestyles. So, I decided to book an appointment. When I asked my doctor, he was shocked and told me he would be very surprised if I had low testosterone levels.

He was wrong.

The test revealed that I had low testosterone. This came as a huge shock to me and really made me think about my health as a whole. I assumed I was taking good care of my body, but I was wrong. This meant I needed to make some changes.

As a part of my plan to increase my testosterone naturally, I started working out in the afternoons when I had more energy. Also, since I was used to going to the gym, it had become a habit, so I didn't need to go first thing in the morning anymore. Instead, I wanted to use this time in the morning for writing and work since it was my most productive time of the day.

On top of all this, I wasn't sure how I wanted to spend my time. Did I want to focus on business? Women? Fitness? Travel and relaxation?

So it was time for a new morning routine.

Now, my goal was to get *better* workouts -- boost my testosterone, get more energy, etc. I was confident that I would go to the gym because I had instituted the habit.

I realized there were some mindsets and limiting beliefs that were holding me back. I felt like I needed to figure out what it was I wanted to do. I felt insecure, and sometimes unsatisfied, but I wasn't sure why. I wanted to dig deep and discover these limiting beliefs. In order to do that, I needed to identify my irrationalities and what they stemmed from so I could proceed with what's most rational.

I realized through a few days of experimenting/testing that I get my best writing done about 1.5 hours after waking up. Writing was critical to me at that time.

Previously, I spent my mornings at the gym. But I found that doing this made it hard to take advantage of peak mental energy which was early in the morning. I realized that I had more physical energy later in the day and more mental energy about an hour or two after waking up.

Then, I found the perfect morning routine that helped me accomplish my exact intentions.

Morning routine #2:

6:00AM: Wake Up To Music, Drink Water
6:15AM: Let My Mind Wander
6:45AM: Write Down 10 Ideas
7:00AM: Journal
7:30AM: Write

8:15AM: Most Important Work Task

Wake up to music

6:00AM

This is the same as my first morning routine. I've woken up this way the last two years and see no need to change it. That's the beauty of trying things out yourself. It may take some time to figure out what works, but once you find it, you can keep the habit for as long as you want. In this routine, I turn off my alarm clock shortly after it goes off so I can hear myself think. Having music playing can make it difficult to relax, focus, and think.

I've learned that drinking caffeine first thing in the morning has some negative consequences. Since I've stopped drinking caffeine early in the morning, I've noticed my energy perks up naturally and doesn't drop like it does when I drink caffeine. I still drink caffeine later in the day. It seems drinking moderate amounts of caffeine during the day is quite healthy for most people.

Let My Mind Wander (Meditation)

6:15AM

This is my form of meditation. I don't focus on my breath, I don't listen to a guide, I just sit and think. Sometimes I think about really weird things. Other times I think about very important issues in my work and personal life.

Sometimes I write down whatever it is I'm excited about at the time. Other times, I just think about random memories from the past. It's hard to explain, but I really just zone out and ruminate. Some people may consider this meditation, but I don't care about labels. I do it at the beginning of the day because I used to never have time later in the day to do this.

Write Down 10 Ideas

6:45AM

Again, this is the same practice as routine #1. However, I do find it more challenging early in the morning, which means I'm only flexing the creativity muscle even more. Writing down ten ideas helps my creativity and helps me me be an idea machine. As you can see, this is a fantastic ritual that I purposely kept in my morning routine.

Journal

7:00AM

After writing out my ideas, I hand write in my journal. The purpose of this is to clear my mind. Once I get it out onto paper, it's out of mind. Sometimes I just write about my worries. Other days, I just dribble out my complete stream of consciousness.

It feels surprisingly good, plus it exercises my writing muscle. My morning journal usually doesn't turn into anything I publish, but occasionally it has lead to the formation of a blog post.

At the end of every journal entry, I express gratitude. Expressing gratitude is valuable because it reminds me of how good I have it. It makes small things that are stressing me out seem insignificant.

I will express gratitude about anything - big or small - significant or insignificant. Past items of gratitude have included living in New York, being able to stream music for free online, my family, access to great food on demand, a book I was reading that I enjoyed, and many more.

Similar to how coming up with ten ideas in the morning has lead to coming up with many more ideas throughout the day, expressing gratitude in the morning has lead to more feelings of gratitude throughout the day. I take notice of the things I appreciate instead of always focusing on what's stressful or what I dislike.

You can learn more about how to journal and how it can help you in chapter 10 of this book. I dive deep into how to do it and what to write about.

Write

7:30AM

Since I've spent the last thirty or so minutes writing out my ideas and thoughts, now it's time to write something more structured. This is when I bang out my blog posts, work on my books, and write my most creative stuff of the day. I've found that I am most creative early in the morning, specifically 60-90 minutes after I wake up.

Everyone is different, but some of the smartest business owners and entrepreneurs out there also do their creative work in the morning.

Most Important Work Task

8:15AM

By this time, I've started to tackle my work tasks (same as routine #1). I've already gotten some writing done, so I'm usually feeling extremely productive. It's pretty crazy how powerful momentum can be early in your day. I found that when I'm productive early on, I only want to be more productive afterwards.

For example, as soon as I'm finished writing, I feel great. I want to keep up my momentum by banging out my most important work tasks.

Contrast that with waking up and checking Facebook every morning. After I check Facebook, I'll be curious to check Instagram, then Twitter. Next thing you know I'm finding every excuse there is not to get my work done.

Key Takeaways

I thought I was in great physical shape, but a shocking visit to the doctor created some urgency: I needed to intensify my workouts.

I moved my workout to the afternoon for two reasons. The first is that I had more energy later in the day. The second was that I was able to take advantage of my peak hours of creativity (in the morning) to be more productive. It was a win-win.

At this time, I also realized my insecurities. I found out that I was afraid of failure, nonconformity, and inertia.

This morning routine helped me gain some self knowledge and improve my creative muscle. I definitely noticed a difference in both.

At one point, a friend even asked me,

"Hey, you come up with a lot of ideas, don't you?"

He didn't realize it, but that was a HUGE compliment. I knew I was doing something right if people were telling me that.

I discovered that I got my most productive work done about 90 minutes after waking up, so I made sure that I was writing every morning exactly then.

The rituals I kept from routine #1 were waking up to music, writing down 10 ideas, and going to the gym everyday (even though I changed the time of day). This gave me amazing benefits, so why would I change something that's working?

Life was pretty good, I couldn't complain. Because spent every morning letting my mind wander, journaling about my thoughts, and writing, it allowed me to realize what I wanted to do with the rest of my life: earn money to support my future family, build a big business, and have the ability to live/travel wherever I want and whenever I want. On top of this, I learned that I wanted to help others do the same. With these goals in mind, I was able to gain some momentum.

My online business was finally bringing in some revenue, and it was all passive, too! That meant I had a lot more freedom.

But this feeling of being completely content wouldn't last long...

Chapter 3
My Morning Routine #3: Work Focus, High Energy, and Self-Education

September 2015.

I hopped out of the shower and dried off. It was a Wednesday afternoon, but I didn't really feel like working. Everyday was the same. Wake up, morning routine, and then work.

After two years of hard work, I had finally made some progress in my passive income business, and it felt amazing. I was making money online and this gave me the freedom to wake up and work whenever I wanted. But what's the point of having all this freedom if I'm working every day?

I thought about going to the library to read a philosophy book instead. I went to the library and spent the entire morning reading philosophy. I didn't have a boss to tell me I couldn't. What a liberating feeling it was, watching all the men in NYC speedwalk across the sidewalk with their briefcases in hand. After an hour or so of reading, it hit me.

Suddenly, I thought about my business. I had put my insecurities behind me and gained control over my emotions, but was I getting too comfortable? Was reading this book helping me take it to the next level? Definitely not.

Routine #2 allowed me to learn a lot about myself. It helped me figure out what I wanted to spend my time on. On top of that, I increased my testosterone back to healthy levels and my mood and energy levels were at an all time high. So, now what? What's next?

I felt accomplished, but I wasn't satisfied. Rather, I was more ambitious than ever. I wanted to take my business to the next level. I had hired a few virtual employees, which meant I had to stay sharp and learn as much as I could to grow my business faster. I had the freedom and no one was telling me what to do when it came to work. This meant it was up to me to keep focus.

I realized that I wanted to be educating myself more and also increasing my focus on work.

I love the following routine because it helps me achieve peak energy, increase my productivity, and reduce my overall stress levels. These were the three things I was more focused on, so this morning routine helped me do just that. If your goal is to concentrate on work, reduce stress, and write (or create), then this morning routine should provide an excellent base for just that. If you're working on something, whether it's a startup, a blog, or a restaurant, this routine will help you achieve your goals.

Morning routine September 2015

7:00AM: Wake Up and Drink Water
7:10AM: Stretch, Breathing Exercises
7:20AM: Read or Listen to a podcast
8:05AM: Write/Work on most important task
11:30AM: Go to the Gym
1:00PM: Get to Office

Wake Up To Natural light
7:00AM

This is the same as routine #1 and #2. However, recently I've been waking up without an alarm clock. It's been amazing. I wake up feel refreshed and energized to start the day. I wake up anytime between 6:30 and 7:00. I know it's time to wake up because my body tells me to.

Instead of consuming coffee right away, I drink 16-20 oz of water. This helps me stay hydrated early on and also wakes me up.

I also keep my four biggest/most important tasks written down on a piece of paper write next to my clock. This motivates me to get the hell out of bed and be productive. It's a small hack, but a great one.

Stretch and Breathing Exercises
7:10AM

Once I'm done hydrating, I do a few stretches. The first one is simple. I bring my arms up over my head with my palms facing out. Then, while squeezing my shoulder blades and sticking my chest out, I slowly bring my arms down to each side while slightly bending my elbows.

As I do this, I try to focus on my breath as much as I can. I don't try to push myself too hard, the goal of this is to get my blood flowing while concentrating on my breath.

I also breathe in deeply for three to five breaths.

After I finish by deep breathing, I review my five year goals to remind myself what I'm working towards. My goals are to:

1) Have $1 Million in assets
2) Have 24/7 determination, focus, energy, discipline and optimism
3) Have the ability to travel or live wherever I want, whenever I want, and however I want
4) Be a mentor to people like me who want to follow a similar path.

Reviewing these gets me motivated to start my day, instead of falling back into bed. It makes me think about all that I can accomplish in life and how enjoyable it will be once I do. This gives me a boost of energy and mood.

Write Down 10 Ideas
6:20AM

This is exactly the same as routine #1 and #2. It's a great habit and I don't plan on removing it from my morning routine anytime soon.
However, since it's become a long term habit, I don't feel the need to do it every single day. Sometimes instead of writing down ten ideas, I'll read or listen to a podcast/audio book instead. I drink tea while I'm doing this.

Write/Work on Most Important Task

7:05AM

I try to publish one piece of content everyday. That means I need to be creating content everyday.

Whether it's a blog post, a book, or a course outline, the morning is the best time to write.

Writing doesn't make time for you; you've got to make time for writing. If you don't, it'll never get done amidst the thousands of other tasks you will encounter during the day.

Recently, writing has been my most important task. I've been working on writing this book as well as several others.

I currently use Asana to keep track of all my tasks and projects as well as my employees. Just having it somewhere is great, as it allows me not to worry about remembering anything, because I know it's all written down.

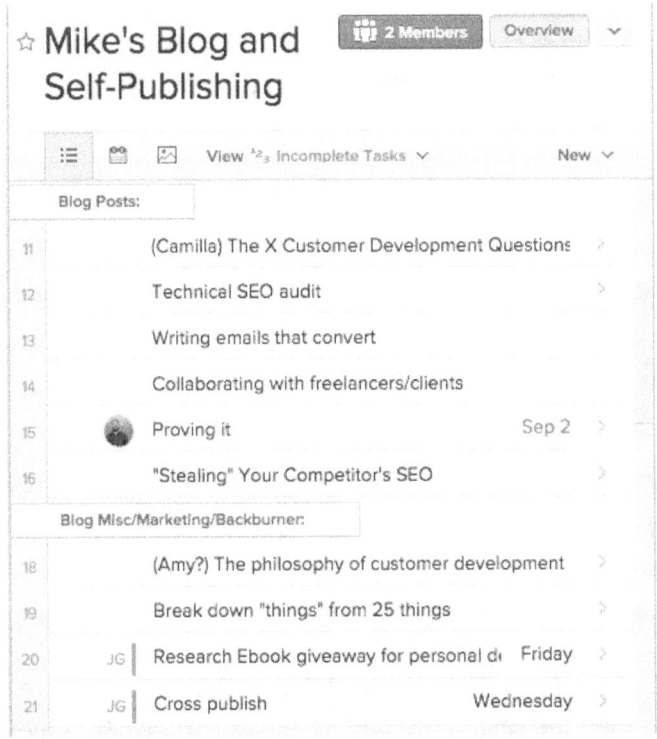

☆ Mike's Blog and Self-Publishing

2 Members Overview

View ¹²₃ Incomplete Tasks

New

Blog Posts:

11	(Camilla) The X Customer Development Questions
12	Technical SEO audit
13	Writing emails that convert
14	Collaborating with freelancers/clients
15	Proving it	Sep 2
16	"Stealing" Your Competitor's SEO

Blog Misc/Marketing/Backburner:

18	(Amy?) The philosophy of customer development
19	Break down "things" from 25 things
20	JG	Research Ebook giveaway for personal d₁ Friday
21	JG	Cross publish	Wednesday

Writing down your tasks and to-do list is a great way to increase productivity. In fact, I would argue that it's inefficient not to have a to-do list. When you wake up everyday without a to-do list, there's nothing stopping you from spending thirty minutes on Instagram or from watching an hour of cat YouTube videos. It's easy to get distracted when you don't have a defined task that you need to do.

I went crazy my first few months without a "real boss". Everyday, I would wake up and not know what the heck to do. Prioritizing my time was difficult.

Now, I use the app Evernote to write down ideas that aren't urgent while I'm on the go and want to remind myself of later (potentially to write more about).

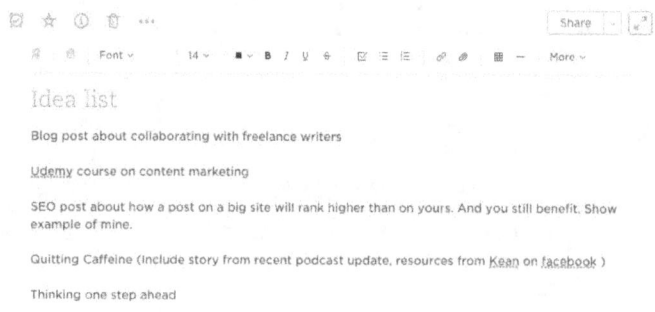

If it's not urgent, I send it to Evernote. If it's an urgent, specific task, I add it to my Asana task list using the mobile app.

As I take a look at my tasks for the day, it allows me to plan the rest of the day. It reminds me what I have to get done. That way, if I find myself getting distracted, I know I should be doing X,Y,or Z because it's on my to-do list. Even if I don't follow the list exactly, I like having it as a guide so at least I know that I have options.

On Monday, I set goals for the week. Sometimes I do this on Sunday night. I set my goals based on what's currently on my task lists and by looking at my monthly and weekly goals. Having weekly goals is a great way to stay focused and also keep track of what you have accomplished. When you check something off your list, you feel satisfied that you have achieved a goal, no matter how small. This then feeds your motivation to be even more productive and maybe tackle those bigger tasks.

Go To The Gym

11:30AM

By this time I usually feel a little bit stressed or overwhelmed so I take a break to decompress. Often I have a lot of energy at this time as well, so I can workout for longer. The gym is usually not crowded at this time compared to 5PM. After my workout, I eat a huge lunch, shower, and get back to work.

Head to Office

1:00PM

I work from home in the mornings, but I like to get out of the house in the afternoon. While I'm able to get work done at home, I feel like it's not great for my creativity to work from home all day.

Two days a week, I work out of an office. The other days, I head to a coworking space or a coffee shop. When I walk, I listen to music or a podcast which allows me to change my focus and take a break from whatever project I was working on.

Key Takeaways

If you gave me a check for a million dollars today, my morning routine wouldn't change a single bit.

Maybe I'd wake up in a slightly nicer bed in a nicer house, but the rest would be the same.

Stretching right after waking up has been a lifesaver. Who would have thought that a few minutes of stretching could helped me stay more relaxed and stress free throughout the day?

As I became more focused on work, the more I read and educated myself, the better and more confident I felt.

I also started working from home every morning and going to the gym around 11:30AM before lunch. Going to the gym was a great break in my day that that allowed me to let off some steam, make sure my workouts had the best intensity, and enabled me to focus afterward.

I also cut out coffee completely. I feel great knowing I figured out how to maximize my energy even without coffee.

I finally found the perfect routine. It helped me learn and improve on a daily basis, and my energy levels were higher than ever. I'm not sure how long I'll keep this routine, but for now, it's perfect.

Chapter 4
The Night Routine

Though this book is about morning routines, your night routine is not to be overlooked. After all, this is where your morning routine truly begins. If you don't have a proper night routine, then no matter how much time and energy you put into your morning routine, it's not going to work.

Flashback to fall 2013.

It's 11:45PM and I'm just getting home. I toss my bag on my bed. It bounces off and lands on the floor. I cringe. My laptop is in my bag. Those happy hour margaritas may be affecting me more than I realize.

By the time I shower and tuck myself into bed, it's well after midnight. This week was going to be the week where I "got my life back together." The week where I wake up early and go to the gym everyday. I browse email and Facebook. Next thing you know, it's 3:00AM and I wake up. My phone's on my chest, I realize that I fell asleep with the light on.

The first alarm sounds at 6:00AM. I hit the snooze without even thinking. I can't even get out of bed, how am I going to make it to the gym?

If you think you can implement a rockstar morning routine without cleaning up your nighttime routine, *you're horribly mistaken.*

First off, you need to have a bed time.

"But I'm not a child, I'm an adult. Why do I need a bedtime?"

Do sergeants let their soldiers stay up as late as they want the night before a big day of training? No way. Soldiers need their rest and so do you. If you want to be productive, it's best to establish a night routine. That starts with going to bed at the same time every night. Everyone is different, but you need to get enough sleep each night. If you're too tired and groggy in the morning, your morning routine won't be nearly as effective.

About an hour or two before my bedtime, I eat some fruit, usually some mangoes, pineapple, a banana and/or berries. According to the *New York Academy of Sciences*, bananas have a lot of potassium and Vitamin B6, which is needed to make melatonin. Bananas also ease muscle and nerve tension, helping you feel more at ease.

I also take ZMA (Zinc Monomethionine Aspartate) about an hour before bed, which is a combination of zinc monomethionine/aspartate and magnesium aspartate plus vitamin B6. I don't worry too much about the names, but I know that it helps me sleep and aids muscle recovery (they go hand in hand).

As I approach my bedtime, I make sure to engage in activities that allow me to wind down. For me, that's reading a book or listening to a podcast. I also try to consume light content, so I'll read fiction or listen to a podcast about.

I find it's best to avoid screens for the last hour before I go to sleep. Screens aren't natural, so they can confuse our brains into thinking that it's not time to go to sleep yet. When we look at screens, your brain increases its electrical activity and its neurons start to race, which is exactly the opposite of what you want to do before you go to sleep.

I used to check my email at night right before I went to bed. Looking back, it was a horrible habit to have. Reading an important email right before bed meant my thoughts were consumed by the email. If I didn't respond to it right away, it would require mental energy to think about it, keeping me from winding down.

The important thing is that you value your night routine. Remember that everyone is different, so feel free to try it out and keep track of your mood the following day.

Another great hack you may want to try is a night journal. A few successful people I know write in a journal every night. They write three things they are grateful for. This is a great way to train your brain into appreciating the things in your life. It also allows you to take a step back and give thanks for the areas in your life that you may otherwise take for granted.

A journal is also a great way to get your anxieties out. If you're stressing over something, getting it down on paper helps you see things from an objective perspective, often lessening the severity of the worry. It's also a great way to let out any thoughts or worries that may be consuming you. Your troubles can seem absurd when you write them down.

Another use for a journal is to write out a to-do list for the next day. This is especially helpful if you don't have an employer telling you what to do everyday. I use Asana, so my tasks are already there, but writing out a to-do list for the next day takes away the worry time, and opportunity for procrastination of deciding what to do. It also allows your subconscious to work through the night preparing you for the tasks that need to be tackled the next day. I'll go more into how to journal later on in this book.

A few things I do to wind down at night is listen to a podcast or hang with my lady friend. When I hangout with my girlfriend, I purposely leave my phone outside of my room to avoid the temptations.

Keep in mind I do work late one or two nights per week. Usually a Monday and/or Tuesday. But, my girlfriend is also a workaholic, so it's not a problem. More on that later on this book.

Key Takeaways

No matter how perfect your morning routine is, you need a night routine in place. If you're not getting enough quality sleep, your morning routine will not be beneficial.

The best way to get started is to give yourself a bedtime. Once you have that, choose some relaxing activities to do before bed. Make sure you're not checking email too late, and avoid all screens if possible. Journaling and reading is a great way to wind down before bed.

Chapter 5
Weekend Morning Routine

It's Saturday morning. No need to get out of bed until noon, right? It's the weekend, baby!

No rules, right? Drinking replaces productivity, fast food replaces your salad, and TV replaces a book, right? That's the key to a great weekend?

Not exactly.

I still do some work on the weekends. That's just the life of a workaholic I guess. But, I don't mind it because I genuinely love what I do.

However, I do take it easier on the weekends and treat it differently than the week.

During the weekend, I work on creative and strategic tasks. I enjoy spending a few hours reading and writing. It really depends on my mood, workload, and my energy levels.

I may do some some research. This means I learn something new, read the news, or catch up on articles that I didn't read during the week.

Or, I may do something creative. This means writing, strategizing, coming up with new marketing ideas or brainstorming content ideas, etc.

Just like the weekdays, I have better focus and creativity in the morning. But on the weekends, I find that there is less noise and less distractions early in the morning.

I don't go to the gym on weekends. I enjoy working out, but not that much. I give my body two days to recover and rest. This really depends on you and your body, though. Just make sure to listen to your body and take a break if you feel sore.

I tackle more creative tasks during the weekends. I find it easier to write on the weekends. Maybe because most people aren't working, so I feel less pressure on getting something done. Reading is a good thing to do on the weekends. I love reading because it's pleasurable and it also helps me in various areas of my life. However, it's not directly work related so it's still considered taking a break from my busy week.

Occasionally, I'll have a meeting or two on the weekend. But it usually won't be anything serious. I try not to schedule meetings on the weekends because I want to keep it open. It's important to have fun and be spontaneous every once in awhile. I also try to take a trip and get away on the weekends from time to time because I live in NYC and it's pretty chaotic. But no matter where you live, taking a trip gives you a new perspective when you return.

On Sunday, I usually make sure that I wake up early. This makes it easier to wake up earlier on Monday. Because of this, I never drink on Saturdays. Sundays are good for long term thinking, goal setting and mentally preparing for the week. Most Sundays I will set a workout routine for the week. I'll also do some goal setting.

Goal setting is important because it helps me get to where I want to be as well as track my progress. Without a goal, how can you score? Every Sunday, I take ten or so minutes to write a few weekly and monthly goals and review my previous goals. It helps a lot and I love it. But, some people do completely fine without goals. Others may not need to set goals because their employer does it for them. It really depends on you and your situation.

I always take one day off. When I take two days off, it's not that I feel guilty, but I just feel like I'm not making progress towards my goals. I love my job, and I get excited when I work on my projects. That being said, it's always nice to take a break from everything and just enjoy life.

My weekends really vary depending on my energy levels, work needs, and social life, but I like it like that. Sometimes I'll take a digital sabbath and not use any electronics from Friday night until Saturday night. Other times, I'll get a lot of writing done. It depends on whatever is most optimal for what I'm working on at the time.

If I've been burying my head in one project all week, then sometimes I'll take the full weekend off and not think about it. Then, when I return to it on Monday, I'm refreshed with a new perspective.

The key to my weekend routine is making sure that it doesn't throw me off schedule for my week. On the other hand, sometimes being disgusting on the weekend makes you more motivated to step it up during the week. If you'd rather go crazy on the weekend that's fine, but then I recommend easing back into your morning routine.

For example, if you wake up at noon on Sunday, don't try to wake up at 6AM on Monday. Maybe try waking up at 8AM, and then 7AM on Tuesday, and 6AM for the rest of the week.

Remember that a decent morning routine that you're able to follow is better than a "perfect" morning routine that you're not able to keep up.

In fact, most of this is all about you figuring out what works best for you.

I keep a strict diet during the week. So for me, it's important to have cheat days on the weekend. During the week, I stay away from carbohydrates. The only sugar I have is from fruit.

But on the weekends, I eat whatever I want. Candy, popcorn, chocolate, you name it!

However, the longer I've kept a healthy diet during the weak, the more unappealing crappy food is.

The opposite holds true for me as well. Once I start regularly eating badly, it's harder to go back.

Everyone is different, but I recommend having cheat meals without going overboard for extended periods of time.

Staying productive on Weekend: Why Workaholics Should Mate

Alcoholics make great companions. They're both always drunk and as a result, very "frisky", too. Well, most of the time. They may get aggressive every now and then.

Workaholics pair well with each other as well. Minus the aggression part. I've learned this from personal experience.

First off, workaholics understand each other and have similar priorities. They're both creative, hard working, and, let's be honest, not very "fun".

If they're true workaholics, work is high priority. Work comes before play, before dates, and before social events. That's completely okay, as long as it's mutual. Workaholics shouldn't bother dating someone who's not busy with their work, because the expectations on both sides are not going to line up. The non workaholic is bound to get angry when the workaholic chooses work over a dinner, a movie date, or even sex.

Even if the two people are working on different things, they're both busy. Still, as a workaholic, you are always going to have little breaks where you won't be working. So you may as well spend it conversing or making out than checking Facebook.

Sleepovers are perfect. Both people are tired, possibly too tired for sex before bed. There's nothing worse than leaving your partner aroused but unsatisfied at midnight because you're too tired. But, when both people are tired, there's no problem.

In the mornings, one person can work the other up since workaholics want to wake up early to start the day and get to work. No one will need to rationalize working late at night, and neither person will have to spend much time thinking about what to do when you're not working. And when you take a break and are relaxing with another workaholic, your priorities are similar. This means you'll both probably be talking about work. Only another workaholic would be okay with that.

You can take turn making coffee runs and picking up lunch, and you can possibly even help each other with work related tasks. It's always easier to give advice on someone else's work than on your own. Just be careful not to date a competitor. That could turn out ugly...

Having a companion that is on board for weekend productivity and perhaps some bouts of work is essential to a healthy relationship and also a fun and productive weekend.

Chapter 6
3 Ways To Destroy Your Morning

We've talked a lot about what I do each morning, however what I don't do is equally notable. I know this because I've made these mistakes and experienced the harmful effects.

1.Check Email Excessively.

Email is a time suck and a stressor. It reduces my focus for creative thinking, too. If I'm exercising, email distracts me from my workout. If I'm writing down my ideas or writing a blog post, email is a huge distraction.

I've sat in meetings and spent time with friends while constantly checking my email. It's very disrespectful to the people I'm with and it prevents me from focusing and enjoying the present moment. It's also easier to miss important topics of conversation or subtle social cues that can help you get to know a person better.

I used to use my phone for my alarm clock and I'd keep it right next to my bed. Before I went to bed, I'd check my email. When my alarm went off I would turn over, turn it off, and then immediately check my email before getting out of bed...before even taking a second to hear myself think!

This was a horrible idea. Checking email first thing in the morning inundates my brain with information overload and stresses that I don't actually need to think about until later in the day.

Basically, I was checking email every few minutes from the time I woke up to the time I went to sleep. This meant at night I wouldn't really decompress and it probably affected my sleep quality or kept me awake for longer. Then, in the morning when I checked my email, I would start off my day with a flood of stress. Sounds like an email addiction right? I agree.

Now I don't check email until 9AM. A full three hours after waking up! Guess how many times I've missed an emergency or an important email because I waited three hours to check my email? Not once.

A product called Batched Inbox has allowed me to stop checking email first thing in the morning. I think not checking email early in the morning has had tremendous benefit for me. Sometimes I "cheat" and access my emails, but I do it far less and often much later in the day than I used to. I've had a hard time sticking with this consistently, but it's good productivity porn.

If you constantly check email, you're responding to emails on everyone else's time. If you're checking email every ten minutes, then you're responding shortly after every email arrives. Not all emails require a response within ten minutes. In fact, I would argue that 99% of emails don't require an urgent response. If it was that urgent, then the person would call you.

Instead of overwhelming my brain with email overload, I take some time to relax, settle into the day, and think about how I'm going to spend it. This helps me paint a picture for what a productive day will look like and also gets me excited for the day to come. I also think about my main tasks and what I have to get done. This helps me to be a lot more proactive than reactive.

It may seem like all your emails are urgent, but in reality, they can almost always wait for at least a few hours...often for a few days! I give some people my cell phone number in case they do have something urgent to tell me. Remember way back when when cellphones were actually used as a device to call people when you needed them? Yeah, that still applies today.

The way you start your day can set the tone for the rest of it. The first thoughts that pop into your head can affect the rest of your morning and the rest of your day. If your first thoughts are stressful or negative thoughts, it could hinder you from carrying out the healthy morning habits described in this book.

It's crucial to start your day with positive, motivating, energizing thoughts. That's the reason why I set my alarm clock to play my favorite music in routines #1 and #2. And why I take a relaxing walk to the gym every weekday morning. It's also why I don't check my email first thing after waking up!

After a good night's sleep you haven't checked email in about 8 hours. That's a long time. What if someone was trying to get hold of you? What if someone has a business opportunity for you? What if your website is down and you need to scramble to fix something?

I know it's tempting to check email first thing in the morning. I've been there. And done that. But it's not the best habit to get into. It can scatter your thoughts, shatter your morning focus, disrupt your routine and habits, and potentially throw off the rest of your day. 99% of the time you won't have an email that you actually need to know about at 6 o'clock in the morning! For most people, the emails we get between the hours of 10pm and 10am are not urgent and can wait until the late morning.

If you really need to be reachable, you could give people your cell phone number so they can text or call you or you could have a private email address where you know you will only get emergency emails.

To avoid checking email in the morning, I would recommend not using your phone as your alarm clock. I would also recommend leaving your phone away from your bed. When I used to kept it next to my bed, I would literally check my email seconds after I woke up. The light of the phone would burn my eyes. The stresses of a gazillion emails would scatter my brain and send me off in a stressed panic to start the day - completely out of balance and focus.

It's not the end of the world if you do succumb to the temptation of checking your email first thing in the morning. Don't let it ruin the rest of your day. Accept that it happened. It's in the past now and there's nothing you can do to change it. Just do your best to proceed forward with the best of your morning rituals.

2. Drink during the week.

Happy hours are always happening. There's always a good deal going on at a bar somewhere or a game to watch. But, I've found this detrimental to my morning routine. When I don't drink, I sleep better, feel better, and perform better.

Yes, I usually drink on the weekends, but not excessively. When I do drink, I don't feel guilty about it. I don't feel guilty about it because I work hard during the week. Also, I don't feel bad because it doesn't destroy my morning routine. If a few beers ruins your morning routine, you may want to consider toning back.

I took a month of drinking and it taught me way more than I expected. The entire next chapter is dedicated to just that.

3. Kill yourself if you break the routine.

Remember, this is a morning routine. It's not a law. So, if I break the routine, I don't worry about it too much. I allow myself to adjust as needed.

I listen to my body. If I'm sore, I don't work out. If I'm tired I sleep a little later. I have a social life, and that makes me happy and therefore increases my energy and productivity. So, I allow myself to break my routine for my social life occasionally.

For example, if I go to a concert on a Tuesday, I might sleep a little later on Wednesday, and/or skip the gym. This is completely okay.

Chapter 7
11 Lessons Learned From 30 Days Without Drinking

February 2015.

I didn't realize how hard it would be to stop drinking. I had even taken a month off in January 2014, just 12 months earlier, but it was much harder this time around. I'm not sure why.

I don't think drinking had been a major problem for me...but it certainly wasn't helping. Since I'm always testing new things and experimenting to see what will help me, I wanted to see what not drinking would do.

In New York it's hard not to drink. Almost everyone drinks. Some people drink a lot more than others. Most people in NYC use drinking as an excuse to get together. When you are celebrating a promotion at work, it's appropriate to go out for drinks. When you're feeling somber because you just got dumped, it's appropriate to go out for drinks with your friends. When you're enjoying an exciting evening out, it's appropriate to drink. A wedding? A funeral? A vacation? A sunday brunch? Yup, yup, and yup! It seems to be appropriate to drink alcohol at any occasion.

Apartments are small so no one wants to hang out at home, let alone have people over. A lot of people below the age of 30 have roommates, which makes it even more undesirable.

In NYC here isn't much to do outside. It's a concrete jungle. So whenever anyone wants to get together socially, or even for business, the opener is often, "let's get drinks."

I found myself drinking about 4 nights a week. Not a lot of drinks each night, just a few. But I felt guilty. My body just didn't feel great after a night of drinking, and it was negatively affecting my sleep schedule.

Some nights I would drink a lot and it would make the following day unproductive. Sometimes on the weekends I would stay up really late drinking and it would throw off my sleep schedule.

We learn from a young age that drinking kills brain cells. My habits couldn't have been making me smarter, only dumber.

When I had taken the month of January 2014 it felt like my brain was moving at twice as fast. I was focused and motivated. So I wanted to see if I could do it again and focus my newfound energy on work.

Let's get to the 10 lessons I learned from not drinking alcohol for a month:

1. Better Sleep

I've noticed that I sleep better. I fall asleep a little easier, sleep more consistently through the night and then wake up feeling refreshed. It's nice not waking up and falling back to sleep as much throughout the night. Now I even wake up without an alarm. That feels even better. I used to almost never wake up before my alarm. Now it's happening fairly frequently.

I used to think drinking was good for sleep because it would make me fall asleep faster, but it's not. I might fall asleep faster, but the sleep quality is worse. I simply don't feel as rested in the morning and if I feel groggy, I won't be as productive. I might not even be able to go to the gym or get writing done if I drank too much the night before. So there is a lot of benefit from falling asleep early.

2.Able To Eat More

Alcohol has a lot of calories. It can make you fat if you drink too much. So an additional benefit of not drinking is that I can either lose weight, or replace the calories with delicious food instead.

For me, I wasn't gaining weight while I was drinking and I didn't want to lose weight. So I've started eating more. I eat so much of everything! I add butter to stuff, I add cream to my coffee (when I drink it), and I find ways to add more calories to my meals. But I won't get fat because I'm still consuming less calories than if I were drinking alcohol.

3.Save Money

Drinking can actually be a pretty pricey hobby. In New York, you can easily spend six or seven dollars on a single drink. That adds up. If you have a few of those per night a few times per week, that's a fairly significant amount of money.

When you go out to dinner, sometimes the drinks are more expensive than the meal. Especially if you get a nice bottle of wine.

By not drinking, I save a lot of money. With the additional cash, I can go out to dinner more often, re-invest more money in my business, save, spend it on classes and books to educate myself, or spend it on any of the other activities I enjoy besides drinking.

4. Less Anxiety

Some people, whether they are conscious of it or not, drink to reduce anxiety.

However alcohol actually causes anxiety. There have been studies that show that it does. It's a depressant.

I would get anxious when I started losing control in a public social situation. I would get anxious when I woke up in the morning and couldn't fully remember everything I did.

I was feeling kind of anxious during days seven through twelve or so, but then I felt less anxious.

5. Moderation Is Key

In so many aspects of life, moderation is key. I think drinking is no exception. I don't think I'll never drink again. Presently, I drink about once every two months. And I only have a few drinks each time.

Some people can get wasted and not feel the negative effects the next day. I'm not one of those people.

6. Sober Sex is Still Fun

As I mentioned earlier, my girlfriend agreed to stop drinking for the month with me. I think it was great for our relationship not to drink. We got to know each other on a more personal, more real level.

This is kind of sad and embarrassing for me to say, but having sex while sober was really a comfort zone pusher for me. I have had sober sex in the past, but probably not that much or frequently. Sex is a very vulnerable and personal act. Many people are self-conscious about it.

Most people get some degree of nerves around it. Some people use alcohol to suppress the nerves they have around sex. I think I have done that in the past. I'm glad I had so much sober sex because it really made me more comfortable with myself as well as my partner.

7. Habits Can Be Changed

One of the biggest benefits of not drinking for this long may be that I have lost the habit of automatically reverting to drinking when thinking about what activity to do or how to spend my time. Previously, when I finished work, was planning on getting together with friends, or otherwise had free time, I would revert to asking people to go for drinks.

Over the past several weeks going for drinks has not been an option. I have not given myself the option. When I just finished my month without booze, I hoped that I would maintain this way of thinking even if I decided to drink again (on occasion and in moderation). I expected that in the future I would not give in to drinking as frequently or as easily. I expected that I would rather replace it with some of the activities that I enjoyed doing when I was not drinking.

I was right. Some of the activities I revert to now that I don't drink as much include going for coffee, reading, going out to eat, or going for a long walk in the city. Those activities are obviously much healthier and productive than drinking. I expected that this experiment would have some lasting benefits and it did.

8. Not Drinking Is Not Easy.

Days five through fourteen were the hardest. The first few days were no problem because I had just drank a few days previously so I didn't miss it that much yet. After day twelve or so, I felt fully "detoxed." Then, I started feeling great, having more energy and sleeping better. I never fully "forgot" about alcohol, but it definitely got easier.

When I would see booze I would want to drink it. I actually like the taste of good beer and whiskey, which made it even harder. One morning, I was having breakfast at the counter of Delicatessen, a diner/cafe I like to go to for breakfast in Soho, and their collection of alcohol were right in front of me. It made me a little anxious. But I ignored it. I thought about ordering a glass of whisky on the rocks. But, then I thought about how good I felt without it. I thought about how great I was going to feel the next day. I let it pass. I was proud that I did. I am stronger now for moving past it.

Knowing that I wasn't quitting forever and that I will eventually drink (in moderation) again made it less stressful.

It's socially unacceptable not to drink in some circles. People want to bring you down. Even my mom tried to get me to drink - though she just wanted me to have fun. Especially in a city like New York, where most people drink. I'm working on meeting people who don't drink and want to do activities that don't involve doing something with a drink in hand.

9. Hangovers Are Worse Than I Realized

After not drinking for a while, my tolerance plummeted. The good news was I could have two beers and feel the effects. But it was never worth it, because the hangovers were REALLY BAD.

This just gave me more incentive NOT to drink and added leverage to my no drinking campaign. The hangover makes me realize how bad drinking is for my body. It also ruins my day. I don't want to do that. When I feel tempted to drink, I think about how shitty I will feel for the entire following day, and it helps me to make a more rational decision.

10. Nobody Cares (If You Don't Drink)

I walked into the bar. The smell of booze made me want to order six shots and catch up with everyone. I met up with my friends. I put my hands in my pocket, trying to avoid the awkwardness of not having a drink in my hand.

"Mike, you want a beer?"

Boom. It hit me sooner than expected. And it hurt.

My palms grew sweaty. Should I lie? Should I pretend like I didn't hear him and ignore him? Should I go to the bathroom and pretend I was sick?

None of these lame excuses would work.

"No thanks, man. I'm actually taking a sober night tonight."

He smiled, *"Wow, I'm impressed."* And the conversation was done. Over.

That was it? He wasn't going to interrogate me until I bought a drink? Nope. It turned out that nothing happened. My friend went and bought a beer. I stayed put. I'm not 15 anymore where I get peer pressured into doing everything. I realized quickly that people didn't care if I was drinking or not. They also respected my decision and didn't force me to drink at all. It's true that drinking is common and a lot of people do it, but a lot of my generalizations about the drinking culture proved to be wrong. It was all in my head.

11. Experimenting Is The Only Way To Learn

If you think drinking might be causing anxiety, holding you back from success, or hindering your sleep patterns, try taking a month off of drinking. Test it and see how it affects you. I didn't realize how much I drank until I stopped. You might be surprised at how it affects you.

Not drinking has reduced my anxiety, increased my cash flow, increased my nutrition, improved my sleep quality, improved my relationship, and ultimately increased my focus and energy levels. Drinking has an impact on so many other aspects such as your mindset, energy levels, focus, and productivity. It can really disrupt your sleep which then disrupts your whole day.

Knowing that you can have another drink later in life and that no habit is permanent might take the pressure off quitting for the month. Hopefully you've learned from my experience and give it a try. You can read about it all you want, but the best way to see how taking a break from alcohol affects your life is to give it a try yourself.

Chapter 8
More Life Hacks To Be More Productive and Efficient Than Ever

There is a lot that can influence your productivity aside from just the morning routine. Just because you have an awesome routine doesn't mean you will have an awesome day. Conversely, even if you don't have an awesome routine, you can still have an awesome day. Here's a list of things I'd like to try at some point. For simplicity sake, all of these sections are written in present tense, even though I haven't yet practiced them.

No Meetings Before 10

Mornings are my most creative time, so I want them to myself. I don't want to have any calls or meetings. My main focus should be my work and my own projects. So, I don't schedule anything before 10AM...

More Friends With Similar Healthy Lifestyles

The more friends I have with similar healthy lifestyles, the easier it is to maintain my healthy lifestyle while having fun. For example, sometimes I socialize early on weekends. It's great because I'm not interested in getting blackout drunk on Friday nights. Another example is to do activities that don't involve drinking at night after work. Bowling, mini-golf, darts, chess, etc. These are all games that can be enjoyed sober, and it'd be nice to have some friends to enjoy them with.

Less News/Blog Reading

This can almost always wait. As I talked about earlier, the news isn't worth my time anymore. It's always changing and it's not going to help me a year from now. Blog posts and articles are the same. Though, those can be quite educational. I want to get better at managing my time by bookmarking them and reading them later. If I revisit them later and realize they're not as important as I once thought, that's okay too

Get Outside More

I'd like to go on more walks or at least check out the view from my roof more often. Going outside gets hard in NYC, especially when it's cold in the winter. When I was in Austin I stepped out on my porch because I had one, and it was great. Being outside in the sunshine always puts me in a better mood. I just wish I did it more.

Wake Up Earlier.

Given I do my best work in the morning, I've thought about waking up even earlier. I know that 6:00AM is already early for most people, but I hear about a lot of entrepreneurs who get up closer to 5AM every morning. Many of them talk about getting their main tasks done early in the morning and doing more by 9AM than most people do in their entire day.

That being said, this would be hard to do if I go out on weekends. It'd also be hard for my girlfriend, unless she agrees to wake up at 5AM as well.

Morning Mantra/Affirmations.

A lot of smart people I know and/or follow read a mantra every morning. They claim that it reminds them of their values and priorities. Reading a mantra or some affirmations would help remind me of my core values It would also help me prepare for the day and get motivated to get to work.

My friend wrote a blog post about his morning mantra, and it definitely got me thinking about adding one to my morning routine. In this post, he also includes his morning mantra, which gives me a rough idea of what I could use for mine.

Given my focus now is on improving my energy, discipline, mood, focus, etc, I would want to have motivational mantras about my capabilities and strengths, gratitude, and thinking about my long-term goals.

Meditate.

I don't meditate. Here's why:

Meditation is commonly recommended by mental and physical health professionals, and it seems like something I would enjoy and benefit from. But I didn't. I tried it for 10 minutes every day, and after a month, I really didn't notice much benefit. I only felt like I had 15-30 minutes taken out of my day. In fact, I felt like it was even causing me to be more stressed at times, since those 15-30 minutes could have been spent doing something productive.

It's definitely possible that I just needed to stick with it for longer, or maybe I wasn't practicing it properly. But after months of regular practice I didn't feel a difference.

Instead, I've found journalling in the morning and free thinking at night to be valuable. Nothing helps me clear my mind the way journalling does. Journaling helps me reduce stress and anxiety and feel more present and grateful way more than meditation ever did.

In addition to journalling, I regularly give myself about 30 minutes to an hour to just listen to myself think. I let my mind wander. I don't try to control my thoughts. I just go. I found this quite relaxing as well. Similar to meditating, I acknowledge my thoughts and emotions rather than trying to control them.

Mediating isn't always necessarily controlling your thoughts and focusing on "nothing". The act of meditation can be many things, actually. Whether it's focusing on one word or a mantra for 30 minutes straight, simply observing your breath, or even being aware of your thoughts.

A lot of people give up on meditation because they set wrong expectations and assume they're not making any progress. As a result, they get frustrated. The reality is that they are making progress, just not in terms of the specific goal they were searching for.

By journaling, I accomplish many of the same goals that meditation does. I'm able to take a step back and take a break from everything. I acknowledge my emotions, fears, worries, and anything else that may be hidden deep in my mind.

By writing all of these things down, I'm subconsciously become an "observer" of my own thoughts. This helps me see them from an objective point of view the same way talking about a problem out loud with someone helps you realize the best solution. Often times, once I write down my worries, I realize how ridiculous they are.

Chapter 9
7 Surprising Benefits of Writing Down 10 Ideas Everyday Like James Altucher

If you noticed, writing down 10 ideas everyday was one of the rituals that I kept in each of my morning routines. Why? It was extremely beneficial, and it only takes a few minutes every morning. I've recommended it to some friends and they've thanked me and told me that it has changed their life. I'm not making any promises, but hopefully this chapter will give you a better idea of the benefits of writing down 10 ideas everyday.

Writing down 10 ideas every morning? I mean, what's so valuable about ideas?

My initial skepticism has turned to advocacy as the benefits, although unforeseen at first, have been profound. Below are 7 ways I've benefited from writing down 10 ideas every day like James Altucher.

1. It Strengthens My Idea Muscle

When I get to around the 7th idea, I can feel my brain start to sweat. Similar to how your body starts sweating when you're doing the last repetition of a set of bench presses. It used to be around the 4th or 5th idea that my brain would start sweating. But since I've strengthened my idea muscle, now it's the 7th or 8th.

Like lifting weights at the gym, pushing yourself to come up with ideas makes you stronger. The benefit of writing down 10 ideas every day is not just the ideas themselves. In fact, at least a couple of my ideas are usually terrible ideas that I will never think about again. One of the biggest benefits is that it has strengthened my idea muscle. And as a result…

2. I Have More Ideas Throughout the Day

The ideas don't stop flowing when I write down my 10th idea, put away my notepad, and open up my laptop. They keep flowing throughout the day.

I find myself thinking of business ideas, marketing ideas, and more, during the course of my day. It seems that by taking time to generate ideas in the morning, it keeps happening throughout the rest of the day.

3. Some of the Ideas Are Really Valuable

(Most) ideas are a dime a dozen...but the best way to come up with ideas that are worth more than a dime is to come up with more ideas.

10 ideas per day x 365 days per year = 3,650 ideas. If just one or two of those are great idea, you can be very successful. If 10-20 of them are "pretty good," that can move the needle significantly.

By coming up with more ideas, I increase my chances of having good ideas. I don't execute on all of the ideas, but some of them I do. For example...

4. I Wrote My Own Job Description

I had an idea for a friend that I thought could improve his business. So I gave him the idea. He liked the idea. Then he paid me to do it.

The next evolution of my 10 ideas practice will be to come up with more ideas for other people, and then send them the ideas. It seems like an amazing way to network. Providing value to people up front instead of asking for their time like everyone else is.

5. It Gives Me Clarity in the Morning

I get millions of emails per day. Everyone is always busy. It's easy to get wrapped up in everything and never have time to think about the big picture.

I've found it extremely beneficial just to pause and listen to myself think. Give myself time to be proactive instead of reactive, and to think long-term.

Often when I sit down to think about ideas around one topic, I end up having ideas about another topic. My idea list might be marketing ideas or ways to improve my business, but while I'm writing down those 10 ideas, I'll start having ideas about other things…like new business ideas, people I should introduce to each other, and ways other people could improve their own business.

6. It Builds Momentum To Start The Day

Pushing through the sweat and writing down the 10 ideas starts my day off with a win. This small win gives me momentum to start tackling bigger challenges through the rest of the day. I experience the pride of overcoming a small challenge and it re-affirms that I can accomplish larger objectives.

7. It Brings Me Confidence

Despite the sweat, I'm able to come up with 10 ideas every single day. Like I mentioned earlier, 10 ideas per day x 365 days per year = 3,650 ideas pear year. And if I keep coming up with 10 ideas every day for the next 10 years I will have 36,500 ideas.

Coming up with 10 ideas every single days gives me affirmation that I'm an idea machine. That I will never stop being able to come up with ideas. That I will always be able to think of even more ideas. It reminds me that I have endless opportunities to create value.

How to Write Down 10 Ideas

Step one, get a notepad and a pen or a pencil. Step two: Write.

"But what should I write about?"

Anything.

It's not about the ideas you come up with, it's about the process. It's about sitting there and feeling "stuck", but powering through anyway and coming up with ten ideas.

Here is an example of some ideas to brainstorm:

-Whatever challenge you're currently facing: 10 ways to overcome it

-10 rap songs Barack Obama should write

-A long term goal you haven't had a chance to focus on: 10 ways you are going to take action

-10 ideas that person X can improve his life/business/house

-10 ways your city's environment could be improved

-10 business ideas for 60 year olds past retirement

Do you get the point? It can be about ANYTHING. Once you get started, you'll realize that there are certain areas in your life and profession that require brainstorming. When that becomes the case, use your list of ten ideas in the morning as time to brainstorm for your specific project. If you write ten ideas a day consistently, you'll start to see some amazing results.

If you want, think of a theme the night before and write it down. When you do this, your subconscious is doing the work for you while you sleep. You can also write an idea list of themes. That way, you have plenty of themes to choose from going forward.

If the idea stays in your head for weeks after, chances are you should be acting on it. If you forget all of your ideas, that's okay, just forget it. You'll have ten more tomorrow.

A lot of people are afraid to fail, myself included. Our society is set up to discourage failure. We are in school from the time we are a couple of years old up until high school, when we graduate at 18. Then we go to college for four more years. Some of us even go to grad school for more years after that.

In school you are either right or you are wrong. Risk taking and experimentation is discouraged. You follow a path and stay with your peers.

When you graduate you get a job. As an entry level employee your job is to complete tasks and to execute on processes. You are not encouraged to think creatively, you just need to do your job. When you are doing your job you are either doing your job or your are not doing your job. You are not supposed to come up with ideas, therefore you're not taught to come up with them.

But if you follow the path and do what everyone else does you will get what everyone else gets. Or maybe less. To get more, you have to take risks.

When you are coming up with ideas, don't be afraid to take risks. When you take risks, there is a likelihood that you will fail. Don't be afraid to fail.

Failure is good. It's a learning experience. It makes you stronger and less afraid to fail in the future. Failing faster gives you more time to succeed. Risk is required for extraordinary success. Failure is possible when you take risk. But you can't succeed if you don't try.

Write down bad ideas. Fail fast. Fail often. The more you fail and faster you fail, the sooner you will succeed.

Chapter 10
How To Journal Your Way To a Stress Free Life

As I mentioned in routine #2, journaling is a great form of therapy. It helped me to be more aware of my thoughts and my emotions and to reduce stress. I strongly recommend giving it a try.

"Thoughts accidentally thrown together become a frame in which more may be developed and exhibited. Perhaps this is the main value of a habit of writing, of keeping a journal,—that so we remember our best hours and stimulate ourselves."
- David Henry Thoreau (via his personal journal)

Do you ever feel like you've got a million thoughts in your mind and you can't get em all out? Ever feel like you need to vent about something but no one is awake to listen?

A journal is a perfect solution to these situations as well as many more.

Most troubles seem absurd when written down. Once you write it down, it's easier to be rational. I often write out my problems, and then I write the most logical and rational solution. When a thought is inside your head, it can sometimes be so closely intertwined with your emotions that you often don't recognize the biases behind it. When you get it down on paper, it can help you see it from an objective perspective. I know this because it's worked for me.

If you're interested in journaling for yourself, here are some tips:

Write down your fears, anxieties, and unhealthy thoughts. This may be difficult; that's okay. Sometimes you may not realize what you are scared of or what's making you anxious. This is another beneficial aspect of journaling, it forces you to dig deep and figure out what's really bothering you.

The best time to journal is in the morning or at night. Our days are busy and it's hard to keep a schedule. However, every night we go to sleep and every morning we wake up. So, if you journal at the beginning or the end of the day, it's easier not to miss.

You can also journal only when you're feeling stressed. It feels great to get your thoughts out.

When you do this, don't worry about grammar or style, just write. Let your thoughts flow, don't edit it, and don't take your time to think too much. Just let it go.

Another way you can journal is to express gratitude. At the end of every journal entry, I complete it with one sentence expressing gratitude. I highly suggest this, as it trains your brain to show appreciation for the world around you. There is good in everything, if only we look for it hard enough.

You can do this by simply writing about things you are grateful for. The train? 7/11? Water? Sure, it can be anything! The more you think about this and write about it, the more it'll become a part of your thought process.

Lastly, when you journal, it strengthens your writing muscle. The more you write, the better you'll get at it.

Chapter 11
The Best Way To Get Started and Additional Resources

Getting Started and Establishing Momentum

Accomplishing something small can help you accomplish something larger. The "small win" can give you confidence and help build momentum to go tackle more ambitious objectives.

For example, I consider finishing one chapter or writing 1,000 words as a small win. Whenever I do it, I'm quite proud of it. It can be hard at times, but I view the hardship as a good thing. It just makes me stronger. By celebrating the small victories, I gain more confidence in my willpower because of it.

After a small win in regards to writing, I feel more capable of flexing my willpower muscle in other areas - such as working out for longer, staying more focused, avoiding Facebook, waking up earlier, eating healthier, etc.

Start Small

Momentum applies to your morning routine as well. Once you add one thing that helps you feel better, you'll want to keep going and add another ritual.

So, I highly recommend starting small. I suggest making small changes to your morning routine before making big changes. Small changes are easier to implement and stick to than big ones.

If your current routine is significantly different from mine, that's okay. Don't compare yourself to me. Don't compare yourself to your kid, neighbor, or spouse. Compare yourself to the person you were yesterday, and try to improve a little bit everyday.

I would recommend adding just one or two of these rituals at a time and making small adjustments (waking up fifteen minutes earlier) before making larger adjustments (waking up 2 hours earlier).

Don't Just Follow the Pack

Remember that everyone is different. Test and see what works for you.

Don't introduce these all at once. Introduce them slowly. Try one, or a few, or all of these rituals and see which work best for you. I imagine some will work better for you than others. You do not need to replicate this routine exactly if some things don't help you or if there are other rituals that help you more. My words don't have the last say, your body and mind does. So listen to it.

That being said, these rituals have helped me tremendously and I'm confident that if you implement even a couple of these that you will have significantly more energy and be more productive throughout the rest of the day.

And remember that it's okay to take a day off. It's okay if you forget to write in your journal. This isn't a strict law here, it's a morning routine that's meant to help you live a better life. You don't need to be overly hard on yourself.

And that's ok! **Nobody's perfect.**

I allow myself to fluctuate if needed. I try to be as disciplined as possible, but I still take days off. I make exceptions. There is variability in my morning routine depending on other factors of my life.

You don't have to be perfect either. If you're anything like me, applying just a few of these rituals and routines will have a profound effect on your physical health and mental well being. You don't need to apply everything exactly how I describe in order to benefit. The purpose of a morning routine isn't to check it off of your to-do list, it's to increase productivity, energy, and overall health.

Sometimes knowing that you can stray from your routine some days makes it easier and less stressful. If you think to yourself that you can never again have a doughnut in the morning it might make you stressed or unhappy. A better solution might be to commit to only eating a doughnut in the morning once per month. Reminding yourself that at some point in the future you will be able to have a doughnut can reduce the stress.

Also, mindset is crucial. Stay strong. Be in the present moment - accept your past mistakes and forgive yourself. Think both long-term or short-term. In the short-term it would be easier to keep sleeping, but in the long-term it will only hold you back. Take pride in pushing yourself and building willpower.

Remember that it's not about perfection. I've made a ton of changes along the way, but I'm not perfect. Not. Even. Close. My life now is extremely healthy relative to how it used to be, but I'm only human, just like you.

Lastly, try to make the best of every moment. I always try to make the best of every morning and every day, regardless of the circumstances. Even if I oversleep or get stuck in the rain on the way to work, I try to make the most of it. I try to stay in the present moment - not dwelling on the past or worrying about the future - just making the best decisions in the present moment. I hope you do the same.

If you enjoyed this book, it would be awesome if you could leave an honest review on Amazon.

Additional Resources: It Doesn't Stop With A Morning Routine

Having a morning routine is amazing, but it can also serve as the perfect stepping stone to improve other aspects of your life.

For example, have you always considered cutting alcohol out of your life but never given it a try? Or, maybe you're trying to control email and social media? Did you know about the incredible benefits of journaling?

This book includes dozens of other hacks worth trying for those of you interested in improving your overall health, productivity, creativity, and more. If you're interested in even more personal development hacks, I've written two other books that I think you'd love.

Lifehacks Newsletter

Join my community as I share my best secrets, practices, and lessons learned in order to live a better and more efficient life.

Learn about lifehacks such as:

- *How to optimize your your productivity-*
- *How to maximize creativity*
- *How to overcome procrastination as I share my best ideas*
- *How to deal with nonconformity*
- *And more!*

No B.S., just actional advice from real life experiences.

Sign up for free at mfishbein.com/life-hacks-newsletter

67 Business Productivity Apps to Make Life Easier, Maximize Your Time and Get Stuff Done:

Do you feel like you're wasting time because you don't know exactly which apps to use?

The technology we have available at our fingertips for little or no cost is truly amazing. It's never been easier to increase productivity, make life easier, manage time, and automate your business marketing!

The 67 Business Productivity Apps in this book can help you maximize and optimize your marketing, blogging, writing, entrepreneurship, and daily life outside of business. Buy the book at mfishbein.com/productivityapps

77 Lifehacks: How to Get More Energy, Increase Productivity & Be Happy:

Do you feel like you should be doing more but **you don't have the energy?** Are you looking to **improve your mood and productivity?**

Do you want to live a better life and do more exciting things?

If so, then this book is for people like you. People who want to boost their mental energy. People who want **more excitement and positivity in their life**, but aren't sure how to do so. Check out the book at mfishbein.com/77lifehacks and add more excitement and positivity to your life.